PUT YOUR FAITH TO WORK

Yea, a man may say, Thou hast faith, and I have works: shew me thy faith without thy works, and I will shew thee my faith by my works.

James 2:18

by

Franklin N. Abazie

Put Your Faith To Work
COPYRIGHT 2017 BY Franklin N Abazie
ISBN: 978-1-945133-24-4

All right reserved. This book or any portion thereof may not be reproduced or used in any manner whatsoever without the express written permission of the publisher, except for the use of brief quotations in a book review. All Bible quotes are from King James Version and others as noted.

Published by: F N ABAZIE PUBLISHING HOUSE- aka, Empowerment Bookstore.

That I may publish with the voice of thanksgiving and tell of all thy wondrous works.
Psalms 26:7

To order additional copies, wholesales
or booking:
Call the Church office (973-372-7518),
or Empowerment Bookstore Hotline (973-393-8518)

Worship address:
343 Sanford Avenue Newark New Jersey 07106
Administrative Head Office address:
33 Schley Street Newark New Jersey 07112
Email:pastorfranknto@yahoo.com
Website www.fnabaziehealingministries.org
Publishing House: www.fnabaziepublishinghouse.org

This book is a production of F N Abazie Publishing House.
A publication Arms of Miracle of God Ministries 2017.
First Edition

CONTENTS

THE MANDATE OF THE COMMISSION iv
ARMS OF THE COMMISSION v
INTRODUCTION vi

CHAPTER 1
1 Action Orientated Faith 1

CHAPTER 2
2 The Force of Faith 17

CHAPTER 3
3 The Help of Faith 21

CHAPTER 4
4 Prayer of Salvation 36

CHAPTER 5
5 About The Author 44

THE MANDATE OF THE COMMISSION

"The moment is due to impact your world through the revival of the healing & miracle ministry of Jesus Christ of Nazareth."

"I am sending you to restore health unto thee and I will heal thee of thy wounds, said the Lord of Host."

ARMS OF THE COMMISSION

1) F N Abazie Ministries-Miracle of God Ministries (Miracle Chapel Intl)

2) F N Abazie TV Ministries: Global Television Ministry Outreach

3) F N Abazie Radio Ministries: Radio Broadcasting Outreach

4) F N Abazie Publishing House: Book Publication

5) F N Abazie Bible School: also called Word of Healing Bible School (W.O.H.B.S)

6) F N Abazie Evangelistic Ass: Miracle of God Ministries: Global Crusade

7) Empowerment Bookstore: Book distribution

8) F N Abazie Helping Hands: Meeting the help of the needy world wide

9) F N Abazie Disaster Recovery Mission: Global Disaster Recovery

10) F N Abazie Prison Ministry: Prison Ministry for all convicts "Second chance"

Some of our ministry arms are waiting the appointed time to commence.

INTRODUCTION

This publication is a book designed for action oriented men and women, to take *proper action in faith* concerning their destinies. Our *faith in God* must be demonstrated by our *actions in life*. *"Then said they unto him, What shall we do, that we might work the works of God? Jesus answered and said unto them, This is the work of God, that ye believe on him whom he hath sent."* **John 6:28-29**

Our *faith in God* must be evidence in our daily lives. Unless there is *an evidence of the manifestation of what God has done* upon our lives, *what you call faith is fake*. Just like *breading-in and out.* Evangelist Billy Graham stated it in these terms below: *"Faith is taking the Gospel in; works is taking the Gospel out."*

Most of us that claim to have *faith in God*, but lack the evidence, and the manifestation of it. In my opinion our *faith in God* must be demonstrated in the activities of our lives. *"For as the body without the spirit is dead, so faith without works is dead also."* **James 2:26**

This book *Put Your Faith to work* is a book, designed to provoke anyone into taking action concerning their lives. Unless we take action concerning our present situation, our lifestyle will not change. Unless we are determined and take a decisive action concerning our present condition, what we call faith is not faith. *"By faith Noah, being warned of God of things not seen as yet, moved with fear, prepared an ark to the saving of his house; by the he condemned the world, and became heir of the righteousness which is by faith."* **Hebrew 11:7**

It is written, *"But without faith it is impossible to please him: for he that cometh to God must believe that he is, and that he is a rewarder of them that diligently seek him."* **Hebrew 11:6**

What then is Faith?

In my own simple definition, *faith, loosely defined means taking responsibility for the outcome of our lives*. This implies taking genuine action necessary to change our finances, marriage, education, career, e.t.c. For *faith without action is ineffective (dead)*.

Our faith in God must become evidence of the hand of God upon our lives. Our faith in God must be seen as the proves and evidence of the manifestation of the power of God upon our lives. It must be seen like a mirror reflection upon our lives. Every time you believe the word of God it must become an evidence upon your life.

In this publication I have explained how to demonstrate our faith in God by the application of well calculated relevant action in life. One man said, *"if you failed to plan, you have planned to fail."* As you go through the pages of this small book. I urge you to neglect my grammar, but pay attention to the context of the text. God will use this material to move you into successful action in *Jesus Mighty Name*. Amen.

Happy reading!

~DO YOU KNOW HIM?

It's very tough to introduce anyone you do not know very well. Unless you know me very well, you have little or nothing to say about me. Unless you know God you have little or less to say about him. It is written, *He made known his ways unto Moses, his acts unto the children of Israel.* **(Psalm 103:7)**

How do I know him?

You must repent your sins and be born again.

1) Acknowledge that you are a sinner and that He died for you. (Romans 3:23)

2) Repent of your sins. (Acts 3:19, Luke 13:5, 2 Peter 3:9)

3) Believe in your heart that Jesus died for your sin. (Romans 10:10)

4) Confess Jesus as the Lord over your life. (Romans 10:10, Acts 2:21)

Now repeat this Prayer after me

Say Lord Jesus, I accept you today, as my Lord and my savior, forgive me of my sins wash me with your blood. Right now, I believe, I am sanctified, I am save, I am free, I am free from the Power of sin to serve the Lord Jesus. Thank you Lord for saving me. Amen.

Congratulations: You are now...

A BORN AGAIN CHRISTIAN.

Again I say to you—

CONGRATULATIONS!

---HE IS OUR CREATOR---

1) We must worship Him, because He is our creator.

2) We must worship Him, because He is sovereign.

3) We must worship Him, because we are made in His image.

4) We must worship Him, because our worship attracts His presence.

5) We must worship Him, for our faith in Him to grow.

6) We must worship Him, to nourish and reactivate our spirit man.

7) We must worship Him, because it activates our faith in Him.

8) We must worship Him, to retain the Joy of the Lord.

9) We worship Him to evict depression, envy, and malice.

10) We worship Him to be happy and to escape strive and hatred.

11) We worship Him to escape bitterness, stress, anger, and misery.

BENEFITS OF OUR WORSHIP

1) Worship is medicinal, it heals our soul, body and spirit man.

2) Worship is supernatural, it position us for constant victory in life.

3) Worship is spiritual, it grants us hope and faith in Him.

4) Worship is a mystery, it keeps us on the winning side of life.

5) Worship is faithful, it gives us encourages us to put us the fight.

6) Worship is strengthening, it reduces the size of our problem.

7) Worship is devotional, it proves our loyalty.

8) Worship is humbling, it proves our meekness before God.

9) Worship is power, it grants us access into signs and wonders.

10) Worship is divine, it accelerates divine intervention.

11) Worship is pleasing, God takes pleasure in it.

12) Worship is a treasure, it catches the attention of God.

13) Worship is rewarding, it brings God into our trials.

14) Worship is reciprocal, it provokes God to act.

15) Worship is glorifying, it magnifies God in our situation.

16) Worship is a blessing, it opens the flood gate of heaven.

17) Worship is our responsibility, it delivers us out of obscurity.

18) Worship is deliverance, it releases us out of captivity.

19) Worship is deeper, God looks for us to prove His divinity.

20) Worship is a reminder, God remembers His promises.

21) Worship is protection, we secure His protection.

22) Worship is unity, it grants us angelic help.

What is Faith?

Although there are so many noted outstanding biblical definitions of faith, I like to define faith as the living word from God, that will provoke the living, and convicting force, inevitable to keep anyone at the same spot or level in life. It is the living force that will make any dummy a living wonder. Faith comes with a living force, that pushes and turns anyone into a living wonder in life. Although Jesus looks for our faith as a point of contact the devil plants fear and doubt to distract and keep us in a stagnant position in life.

What does the bible says about Faith?

We are told, *"And without faith it is impossible to please God, because anyone who comes to him must believe that he exists and that he rewards those who earnestly seek him."* (Hebrew 11:6 NIV). If we must please God our faith must be seen ahead of our life and our works. It is written for "without faith we cannot please him."

How does faith come?

Bible recorded that faith comes by hearing. (Romans10:17) So then faith cometh by hearing, and hearing by the word of God.

How does faith works?

Faith works by love. Galatians 5:6 *but faith which worketh by love.* Faith is *a kingdom mystery that works only by love*. As long as there is no love inside of us, faith in God has no relevance, because it will not work. Yea, a man may say, Thou hast faith, and I have works: shew me thy faith without thy works, and I will shew thee my faith by my works.

GOD IS THE SOURCE OF FAITH

However, we can't take credit for our faith. Scripture explains that the source of faith is in God: *"For it is by grace you have been saved, through faith--and this not from yourselves, it is the gift of God--*not by works, so that no one can boast." (Ephesians 2:8-9, NIV). Recall "Jesus said "Have faith in God." Mark 11:22

MUSTARD SEED FAITH

When the disciples were unable to heal a man with a demon, they asked Jesus, *"Why couldn't we drive it out?"* He replied, "Because you have so little faith. *Truly I tell you, if you have faith as small as a mustard seed, you can say to this mountain, 'Move from here to there,' and it will move. Nothing will be impossible for you."* (Matthew 17:19-20, NIV)

In my own opinion, mustard seed faith means enough faith to take action concerning any prevailing challenge in life.Perhaps you have not also noticed, we all do everything in life by faith. *"It is written for whatsoever is not of faith is sin."* **(Romans 14:23)** You cannot stand still and watch your destiny decay. You cannot stand still and watch others get ahead of you in life. You must be moved today into action. In *Jesus Mighty Name I pray.* Amen.

PRAYER POINT TO PROVOKE THE POWER OF FAITH

"For verily I say unto you, That whosoever shall say unto this mountain, Be thou removed, and be thou cast into the sea; and shall not doubt in his heart, but shall believe that those things which he saith shall come to pass; he shall have whatsoever he saith". Mark 11:23

Holy Spirit of God frustrate and disappoint, every one that is against my life and family, in the name of Jesus.

Father Lord destroy every demonic networks and traps against my progress in life in the name of Jesus.

Fire of God, destroy every demonic projection and curses against my life and destiny in the name of Jesus.

Every spell and curses pronounced against my destiny, break, in the name of Jesus.

Hand of God cage every power militating against my rising in life, in the name of Jesus.

Power of God silent every voice raising a counter motion against my elevation, in the mighty name of Jesus.

Blood of Jesus neutralize every spirit of Balaam hired to hinder my life, ministry, and career, the name of Jesus.

Fire of God destroy every curse that I have brought into my life through ignorance and disobedience, break by fire, in the name of Jesus.

Ancient of day destroy every power harassing my ministry in the name of Jesus.

Father God deliver me from invincible forces militating against my life and destiny.

Power of God frustrate every coven and demonic network, designed to frustrate and hinder my success in life, in the name of Jesus.

I dismantle every strong hold designed to imprison my talent in the mighty name of Jesus.

I reject every cycle of frustration, in the name of Jesus.

Power of God paralyze every agent assigned to frustrate my life in the name of Jesus.

Finger of God, grant me supernatural speed against all my contenders in the name of Jesus.

By the blood of Jesus, I destroy every familiar spirit caging my life and career.

Fire of God arrest every demonic agents, assigned to police my destiny and marriage.

By the blood of Jesus, I proclaim no weapon fashioned against me shall ever prosper.

Holy Spirit of God break me through and forward in life in the mighty name of Jesus.

God, smash me and renew my strength, in the name of Jesus.

Holy Spirit, open my eyes to see beyond the visible to the invisible, in the name of Jesus.

Father Lord grant me strength and power in the name of Jesus

O Lord, liberate my spirit to follow the leading of the Holy Spirit.

Holy Spirit, teach me to pray through problems instead of praying about, it in the name of Jesus.

Father Lord, deliver me from the false accusation in life, in the name of Jesus

By the blood of Jesus, every evil spiritual padlock and evil chain hindering my success, be roasted, in the name of Jesus.

By the blood of Jesus I rebuke every spirit of spiritual deafness and blindness in my life, in the name of Jesus.

Father Lord, empower me to dominate the enemy of my destiny in the name of Jesus.

Jesus Christ of Nazareth, heal my infirmities in the name of Jesus

Lord, anoint my eyes and my ears that they may see and hear wondrous things from heaven.

Father Lord, anoint me with power and authority to dominate all my enemies in the name of Jesus.

Fire of God roast every giant rising up against my life and career.

Holy Spirit of God destroy all my oppressors in the name of Jesus.

Angels of good new, bring my good news to me in the mighty name of Jesus.

Every strong man holding me down, lose your hold now in the name of Jesus.

I nullify every demonic prediction over my life in the name of Jesus.

By the blood of Jesus, I flush out every polluted deposit of the enemy in my life.

By the blood of Jesus, I paralyze every enemy of my promotion in the name of Jesus.

Father Lord, destroy any power tormenting my life that is not from you.

Holy Ghost fire, ignite the fire of revival in my life.

By the blood of Jesus, I declare victory over every conflicting trial

By the Blood of Jesus, I command the arrest of every demonic spirit, militating against my life

By the blood of Jesus, I proclaimed the blood of Jesus, over every device of the enemy.

By the blood of Jesus, I revoke stagnation and hardship over my life in the name of Jesus.

Holy Ghost fire, destroy every satanic arrangement in my life, in the name of Jesus.

HIS DESTINY WAS THE **CROSS**....

HIS PURPOSE WAS **LOVE**.....

HIS REASON WAS **YOU**....

CHAPTER 1
ACTION ORIENTATED FAITH

Yea, a man may say, Thou hast faith, and I have works: shew me thy faith without thy works, and I will shew thee my faith by my works.
James 2:18

Faith is a living word, with a livingforce that will make anyone a living wonder in life. In my own understanding, knowingly or not knowingly, we all take action in life daily. As people of faith we must become action oriented in life. It is written, *"But without faith it is impossible to please him: for he that cometh to God must believe that he is, and that he is a rewarder of them that diligently seek him."* **Hebrew 11:6**

In Christianity, faith causes change as it seeks a greater understanding of God. Faith is not fideism or simple obedience to a set of regiment rules or mission statements. Before Christians have faith, they must understand in whom and in what they have faith. Without this understanding, there cannot be genuine faith in God, and that understanding is built on the foundation of the believers, the scriptures, and personal experiences of the believer. It is written *"Therefore I say unto you, What things soever ye desire, when ye pray, believe that ye receive them, and ye shall have them."* **Mark 11:24**

In English translations of the New Testament,

the word "faith" generally corresponds to the Greek noun πίστις (pistis) or to the Greek verb πιστεύω (pisteuo), meaning "to trust, to have confidence, faithfulness, to be reliable, to assure."

For so long now, there has always been a prevailing debate concerning action oriented faith people. Often when secular men/women succeed in life, those who are not our regular religious church folks, we tend to argue over how they managed to succeed without coming to church and attending our regular bible study weekly. The answer to this long outstanding argument is action faith. In my own opinion, there must be a desire first, will-power and a corresponding action plan in the life of anyone who proclaim faith in Christ Jesus. It is written, *"For as the body without the spirit is dead, so faith without works is dead also."* **James 2:26**

If anyone has *faith in God-* which is placing *trust in God. When you trust someone, you will obey* them, because you just know they are right and always have your good in mind. There must be a corresponding action in the life of anyone of us who claims to have faith in God. Every time we take action in life, God honors our active action plan. Regrettably, most church folks cry unto God daily but do not take action to change their life. It is written "Verily, verily, I say unto you, He that believeth on me, the works that I do shall he do also; and greater works than these shall he do; because I go unto my Father." **John 14:12**

It is a paradox to me at least, whenever some of us pray and fold our hands, watching and waiting on God to do something for us in life. In my own understanding

Christianity means taking responsibility and in control of our lives. I discovered that time and chance will not change anything for us in life. In the word of president Obama, *we are the change that we have been waiting for.* Nothing changes for us until we are ready for a change. And to be ready for a change we must take action in life.

"Change will not come if we wait for some other person or some other time. We are the ones we've been waiting for. We are the change that we seek."— President Barack Obama

As Christians we are absolutely responsible concerning the outcome of our lives, otherwise we make Him a liar. Remember—"*…God cannot lie.*" **Titus 1:2**

This change, must start from our heart. A change of our mind is the plat form for a change of life. And a changed life, is a life on track to fulfill destiny. *"For as he thinketh in his heart, so is he: Eat and drink, saith he to thee; but his heart is not with thee."* (Proverb 23:7) Unless we genuinely repent and renew our mind, otherwise, we are not ready for success in life. *"And be renewed in the spirit of your mind."* Ephesians 4:23

In my own understanding, to be successful in life we must change our thoughts. For our thoughts, produce our words, and our words determines our action, and our action forms our habits, and our habit designs our character, and our character shapes our future, and destiny. Unless we make up our mind and become responsible in life, nobody will do it for us. God has already done His part, we must wake up and take responsibility for the outcome of our lives.

Chapter 1   Action Orientated Faith

"And be not conformed to this world: but be ye transformed by the renewing of your mind, that ye may prove what is that good, and acceptable, and perfect, will of God." Romans 12:2

In my own understanding, anyone who have confessed Jesus as savior must be organized, and action oriented in life. *Life is a warfare and not a fun fare.* Unless, we become creative and innovative in life, we will remain poor and praying people only. Unless we take responsibilities in life, by taking action, we will remain vulnerable, and cheap to the devil. *"I returned, and saw under the sun, that the race is not to the swift, nor the battle to the strong, neither yet bread to the wise, nor yet riches to men of understanding, nor yet favour to men of skill; but time and chance happeneth to them all."* **Eccl 9:11**

HAVE FAITH IN GOD

"And Jesus answering saith unto them, Have faith in God." **Mark 11:22**

We can only prove genuine faith in God, by becoming responsible people. The manifestation of our faith in God must become evidence with concrete proves of what God has done. Our faith in God must be seen in our ability to create and innovate new technologies in today fast-moving business world. This outstanding statement defines all I have to say about *action faith.* Anyone can believe in God, but without action, there is no true faith, for what am I trying to prove to others and myself. When the bible said that the just shall live by their *faith*, it literally means that the just shall live by the actions they take in their lives. *"Behold, his soul which is lifted up is not upright in him: but the just shall live by his faith."* **Habakkuk 2:4**

In my own simple definition, *faith in God* means *taking responsibility and taking action in life*. This includes works, but mere believing is a mental process, no action is required when we say we believe, but to have *faith in God*, we must implement and demonstrate genuine action in life.

"Thou believest that there is one God; thou doest well: the devils also believe, and tremble." **James 2:19**

I believe in loving your wife and love ones, but unless there is a corresponding action by giving and sharing your time with them, your love for them is impotent. It is written "For God so loved the world, that he gave his only begotten Son, that whosoever believeth in him should not perish, but have everlasting life."

Every proclaimed lover is a bona-fide giver. **"For God so love… He gave."** God proved His love by His giving. Love without giving is dead. Note that "**giving is the action**" Just like that scriptures says, "As the spirit without the body is dead, so faith also without works is dead also." I have no part in-love, without a sincere giving spirit. Believing in God is only a thought, a premeditated concept that anyone can choose to believe in, it is my actions that prove my faith, and it is my actions that will guarantee my desires in life.

If I may say this, taking action in life is the catalyst of faith, it is the vehicle that carries and propels our

Chapter 1   Action Orientated Faith

desires into manifestation.

Our faith in God is examined in the actions we take in life. I say this because action faith oriented men & women are people of exploit. They are the set of men who pleases God in life time. *"Examine yourselves, whether ye be in the faith; prove your own selves. Know ye not your own selves, how that Jesus Christ is in you, except ye be reprobates?"* **2 Cor 13:5**

We must examine our past, and present actions in life, to determine if we are genuinely in the faith. Acclaimed faith people are people of action. For an example, every time we complain, and fear of lack of money in our checking or saving account in life, before taking the corresponding action in life, God leaves us alone. *"We walk by faith, and not by sight,"* every time our action is dependent on our finances, we make our finances our idle-god, so God, will leave us alone to suffer the wickedness of the taskmaster called "money." I see money as a faithful servant but a wicked master.

We are told by the bible that money answered all things, but also that money is the root of all evil in life. Some of us who claim to have faith in God are unable to take genuine action in life to prove our faith in God. We are scared of uncertainty, afraid of the unknown. We paralyze our life and destiny by over analyzing, what will be, what if, and what not.

"A feast is made for laughter, and wine maketh merry: but money answereth all things." **Ecll 10:19**

"For the love of money is the root of all evil: which while some coveted after, they have erred from the

faith, and pierced themselves through with many sorrows."
1 Timothy 6:10

In order for faith to lead to salvation, it must be centered on the Lord Jesus Christ. We exercise faith in Christ when we have an assurance that He exists, and a correct image of His character, and a knowledge that we are striving to live according to His will.

Having faith in Jesus Christ means relying completely on Him—trusting in His infinite power, tapping into His love, compassion, kindness, peace, joy, wisdom, strength, merciful spirit, kindness, endurance, long suffering. This includes believing His teachings. This I mean; believing that even though we do not understand all things, He does. Because He has experienced all our pains, afflictions, and infirmities, He knows how to help us rise above our daily difficulties.

Faith in God means taking action in life. But believing in God does not need action, like we establish earlier above. Anyone can claim they belief in God, or in any higher supreme being, unless we take action in life, it is not faith in my opinion. Faith is the fulfillment His commandment. Remember, *"His commandment are not grievous."* It is through our actions in life, that our faith in God is manifested and sealed by the Holy Spirit of promise. "For this is the love of God, that we keep his commandments: and his commandments are not grievous." 1 John 5:3

Chapter 1   Action Orientated Faith

Genuine faith in God is received at salvation. "For by grace are ye saved through faith; and that not of yourselves: it is the gift of God:," (Ephesians 2:8) The power of faith is our ability to be disciplined and determined to take positive, and successful actions that inevitably changes and transforms our lives and financial well-being. *Faith in God* as the building block of life must be seen upon our lives at any level of breakthrough, we find ourselves operating in. We must always remain thankful and praiseful unto God, but expectant, for the next level change of life.

"That your faith should not stand in the wisdom of men, but in the power of God." **1 Cor 2:5**

"Who are kept by the power of God through faith unto salvation ready to be revealed in the last time." **1 Peter 1:5**

Faith is the channel for the free flow of the power of God upon our lives. And that power is hidden in actions. Everyone who claim to have faith in God must take definite actions to back all such faith. Taking action in life is the plat form to display the power of God.

"And Jesus answering saith unto them, Have faith in God. For verily I say unto you, That whosoever shall say unto this mountain, Be thou removed, and be thou cast into the sea; and shall not doubt in his heart, but shall believe that those things which he saith shall come to pass; he shall have whatsoever he saith." **Mark 11:22-23**

Faith in God and *faith in* our own intellectual and physical abilities will make anyone successful in life. Although *faith in God* is compulsory for us as believers, but we must also consciously develop *faith in our* own several abilities. Everybody is a talent in his/her own unique area of calling in life. Though often most folks do not walk in the area of their calling in life. To *put your faith to work,* you *must have faith* in God and *faith in your own self.* You must be *dedicated, determined, devoted, and make extra personal efforts* in any discipline you chose in life.

Whenever faith in God is properly cultivated, and used, it has a powerful far-reaching transforming effects in our lives.

Such power of faith can transform an individual's life from maudlin, common everyday activities to a symphony of peace, love, joy and happiness. We must all embrace faith in God and taking the necessary action in life as a lifestyle.

It is written, "But without faith it is impossible to please him: for he that cometh to God must believe that he is, and that he is a rewarder of them that diligently seek him." **(Hebrews 11:6)** God has done His part, we must wake up and do our part in life. You are the change you have been waiting for, you are the breakthrough you have been expecting.

Chapter 1   Action Orientated Faith

HOW TO PUT YOUR FAITH TO WORK

1. We must embrace responsibilities.

2. We must be proactive and always plan ahead in life.

3. Whatever the task may be, we must develop possibility mentality in all things.

4. We must develop a lifestyle to be optimistic in life.

5. We must become working class people, there is no place for the lazy man/woman.

6. We must always believe God will help us in life.

7. We must believe in the supply of supernatural favor from God.

8. We must render favor to others around us in life.

9. We must be kind and cheerful people in life.

10. Go learn a new trade or go back to school.

11. We must help others in life when it is in our power or position to do so.

12. We must develop a mentorship relationship and learn from our mentors.

13. You must become problem solvers.

14. We must develop possibility mentality against any challenge of life.

15. Start a sole proprietor business venture.

16. We must become humble in life.

17. Always read a new thing and keep learning in life.

18. We must volunteer in our community if we are in a position to help.

19. We must become creative and innovative in something good.

20. We must maximize our time and talent in life.

21. We must be positive people who believe in God, and also give others the right advice always.

UNBELIEF

" O thou of little faith, wherefore didst thou doubt?"
Matt 14:31

Often some church folks are confused about hindrances to faith. Although physical hindrances are obvious in life, partly because anyone can see, or experience it. There are unseen hindrances like doubt and un-belief that no one can see with the nacked eye. We can only talk about it through the power of the mind. Doubts in God's word and in the validity of God's promises is a hindrance that will exempt and eliminate us from enjoying the riches of His glory. *"Jesus saith unto him, Thomas, because thou hast seen me, thou hast believed: blessed are they that have not seen, and yet have believed."* **John 20:29**

Unbelief is a hindrance to our miracle. Jesus couldn't do miracles because he marveled at their unbelief. (See Mark 6:4-6) As long as we live in doubt we hinder the power of God from flowing into our lives.

We are told by the book of James that "…For he that wavereth is like a wave of the sea driven with the wind and tossed." (James 1:6) Every time we live in doubt we create fear and confusion for our lives. Remember God is a God of order. Our mental system is designed to believe and recognize the doing of the Lord in our lives.

Doubt is has no part in God's original plan. In fact doubt is a device of the devil, and can never be explained, except on the basis of a terrible calamity in our moral nature. One of the primary reason for Peter's doubt was his fleshy nature. Our physical nature is designed to sense fear and uncertainty from afar. This fear creates a tension atmosphere that makes us to panic in the midst of the storm of life. Although carnality is the root of unbelief, we must embrace spirituality if we must prevail against the adversary-the devil.

~FEAR OF THE UNKNOWN

"LOOKING AT THE PHYSICAL THINGS WE SEE"

"While we look not at the things which are seen, but at the things which are not seen: for the things which are seen are temporal; but the things which are not seen are eternal." 2 Cor 4:18

Other hindrances to faith, is "fear of the unknown." By this, I mean to get afraid at the things we see, and feel with our physical eye. Often we get distracted looking at our surroundings, and not to the precious promise of Jesus Christ. Unless we develop *the lifestyle to "walk by faith and not by sight,"* we will never dominate the prevailing challenges of life.

"And when the disciples saw him walking on the sea, they were troubled, saying, It is a spirit; and they cried out for fear. But straightway Jesus spoke unto them, saying, Be of good cheer; it is I; be not afraid. And Peter answered him and said, Lord, if it be thou, bid me come unto thee on the water. And he said, Come. And when Peter was come down out of the ship,

Chapter 1   Action Orientated Faith

he walked on the water, to go to Jesus. But when he saw the wind boisterous, he was afraid; and beginning to sink, he cried, saying, Lord, save me. And immediately Jesus stretched forth his hand, and caught him, and said unto him, O thou of little faith, wherefore didst thou doubt." Matthew 14:26-31

The incident in the above scripture is an example of the power of our surroundings versus the power of the faith in God. There were two things upon which Peter fixed his attention; one was the word " come," uttered by the Lord Jesus, the other was the storms and the waves of sea. Peter was not desperate in faith, for he asked the Lord to bid him to come, but was afraid of his surrounding once he became distracted in fear. Peter never sank until he allowed fear of the surrounding of the sea to capture his heart.

As long as we cast of fear in love, God will always prove himself in our lives in time of need.

~LACK OF PERSONAL CONVICTION THAT GOD IS ABLE

We must not blame anyone for the outcome of our lives. God has done His part. If we must become great in life we must become responsible for the outcome of our lives. We must develop personal conviction in God that regardless of the outcome of our lives God is able to deliver us from it.

"Wherefore, if God so clothe the grass of the field, which today is, and tomorrow is cast into the oven, shall he not much more clothe you, O ye of little faith? Therefore take no thought, saying, What shall we eat? or, What shall we drink? or, Wherewithal shall we be clothed? (For after all these things do the Gentiles seek:) for your heavenly Father knoweth that ye have need of all these things." Matthew 6:30-32

We must develop conviction like the three Hebrews boys. "Shadrach, Meshach, and Abednego, answered and said to the king, O Nebuchadnezzar, we are not careful to answer thee in this matter. If it be so, our God whom we serve is able to deliver us from the burning fiery furnace, and he will deliver us out of thine hand, O king." (Daniel 3:16-17) We must all be convicted and convinced that God is able to do exceedingly abundantly above that we may think or say. I therefore admonish you to embrace living the remaining part of your life by faith. We must cultivate the habit of taking decisive actions in your life.

GUIDELINES TO OPERATE BY ACTION FAITH

1) *We must get an education, learn a trade, and keep an income-driven job.*

2) *We must always plan five years ahead of our future.*

3) *We must develop a budget and save as much as possible.*

4) *We must develop a business mindset, minimize our expenses and invest our money in life.*

5) *We must develop a mindset of success, and embrace an attitude of zero tolerance to failure.*

6) *We must embrace success as a lifestyle and make friends with successful men and women in life.*

CHAPTER 2

THE FORCE OF FAITH

"By faith Noah, being warned of God of things not seen as yet, moved with fear, prepared an ark to the saving of his house…." **Hebrews 11:7**

It is established in the Holy Scriptures that with the force of faith in God, we can move any mountains anywhere. It is written, *"Jesus said unto him, If thou canst believe, all things are possible to him that believeth."* **Mark 9:23**

Jesus said to the tree, "May no one ever eat fruit from you again." He said it loudly enough so that His disciples heard Him. The next day as they began their journey back down the same familiar road, Peter saw that the fig tree had withered from the roots. "Rabbi!" he exclaimed. "The fig tree you cursed has withered!" And with that miracle Jesus began to expound on the subject of faith.

"And Jesus answering saith unto them, Have faith in God. For verily I say unto you, That whosoever shall say unto this mountain, Be thou removed, and be thou cast into the sea; and shall not doubt in his heart, but shall believe that those things which he saith shall come to pass; he shall have whatsoever he saith." **Mark 11:22-23**

The truth is, *our faith in God must move us into action in life* otherwise it's not faith. Everyone who confesses faith but does not take action in life is just confessing a mere word. Faith in God dwell in our action in life. Unless we become action oriented in life we will never make an impact. However, just only *"speaking and believing,"* cannot help us accomplish much in life. We must be action ready as soldiers of Jesus Christ. One prevailing factor of action *faith in God* is that, *action faith* does not *recognize problems*, *rather it* interprets *problems as opportunities*. One great Man of God was asked by New york times. *"Have ever had a problem? He responded maybe it came and I didn't know.* Faith in God is the key to all victorious life, and successful living as far as I know.

The force of faith is a mystery that conquers and turns any obstacle into an opportunity, rather than recognizes threats, and weakness. The reality of *action faith* is that it have un deniable proves. Action faith people are people that hear from God. Therefore, it is impossible to change or sway the mindset of men of action faith in life.

~believing and speaking

"We having the same spirit of faith, according as it is written, I believed, and therefore have I spoken; we also believe, and therefore speak." 2 Cor 4:13

Every time we believe, it is with our heart but when we speak it is with our mouth. So then, if we claim we have faith when we speak and believe without action, our faith in Him is dead therefore. In my understanding *"Believing and speaking go together."* So many people are speaking without believing, and therefore are not getting any positive results life. The truth of action faith means that, it is the faith that can be heard, seen, and touched. *Faith in God* means taking *genuine action in life.*

Often, we wonder when unbelievers (those who do not know God) put their faith to work and become successful in life. We must apply the principles of Jesus Christ if we must become successful in life. *Remember, Jesus said I must work the works of him that sent me, while it is day: the night cometh, when no man can work.* **(John 9:4)** We are warned, *"For even when we were with you, this we commanded you, that if any would not work, neither should he eat."* **(2 Theo3:10)** The bible gave us hope and commanded us to put our faith to work. It is written, *Whatsoever thy hand findeth to do, do it with thy might; for there is no work, nor device, nor knowledge, nor wisdom, in the grave, whither thou goest.* **Ecll 9:10**

The force of faith moved Noah

"By faith Noah, being warned of God of things not seen as yet, moved with fear, prepared an ark to the saving of his house; by the which he condemned the world, and became heir of the righteousness which is by faith." **Hebrews 11:7**

The force of faith moved Abraham

"So Abraham departed, as the Lord had spoken unto him; and Lot went with him: and Abraham was seventy and five years old when he departed out of Haran."

Chapter 2 The Force of Faith

Every time we are moved by *faith in God*, we must always trust God to secure His promises concerning our lives. Some people will not take action in life because they want God to secure the future ahead of their stepping out. *The force of faith* in God does not work that way. We must realize that God uses faith to train us to become strong and effective for useful impact in life. "Unless you have been tried you cannot be trusted in life." As we act on God's Word, we activate the power of God within us, to move mountain, break down obstacles and challenges, and obtain the desired victory in life.

"And Jesus answering saith unto them, Have faith in God. For verily I say unto you, That whosoever shall say unto this mountain, Be thou removed, and be thou cast into the sea; and shall not doubt in his heart, but shall believe that those things which he saith shall come to pass; he shall have whatsoever he saith. Therefore I say unto you, What things soever ye desire, when ye pray, believe that ye receive them, and ye shall have them." **Mark 11:22-24**

The primary function of action *faith in God* is to deal with unforeseen barriers and Satan's wiles and assaults that hinder us spiritually, mentally, financially or physically.

It is impossible to please God bearing grudges against anyone in our heart. Often, whenever we pray, we still experience frustration or feel the pain in our body. The Word of God, is the sword of the spirit to encourage ourselves in difficult times

CHAPTER 3

UNDERSTANDING THE HELP OF FAITH

"Holding the mystery of the faith in a pure conscience."
1 Timothy 3:9

Without the *help of faith in God*, we are helpless to the assaults, tricks, and wiles of the devil. We must recognize *the help of faith* in our daily lives.

As long as we live, we desperately need *the help of faith*, to save the sick, to heal the broken heart, to deliver the captive, to protect everyone that is vulnerable. e.t.c. There is no sick person who will be completely healed without *faith*. "*And the prayer of faith shall save the sick, and the Lord shall raise him up; and if he have committed sins, they shall be forgiven him.*" **James 5:16**

"*And as he entered into a certain village, there met him ten men that were lepers, which stood afar off: And they lifted up their voices, and said, Jesus, Master, have mercy on us. And when he saw them, he said unto them, Go shew yourselves unto the priests. And it came to pass, that, as they went, they were cleansed. And one of them, when he saw that he was healed, turned back, and with a loud voice glorified God, And fell down on his face at his feet, giving him thanks: and he was a Samaritan. And Jesus answering said, Were there not ten cleansed? but where are the nine? There are not found that returned to give glory to*

Chapter 3   Understanding The Help of Faith

God, save this stranger. And he said unto him, Arise, go thy way: thy faith hath made thee whole." **Luke 17:12-19**

There were ten lepers who were cleansed but only one was made whole by faith. In this trial, times that we live in, we all need the help of faith in God. Every faithless person dies before their time." No matter what we all do for a living we all need the help of faith in life. The pilot in an airplane need *the help of faith in God* to land the plane. The driver on the ground need the help of faith in God to safely get to their destination *"...for whatsoever is not of faith is sin."* Romans 14:23

THE HOLY SPIRIT IS THE HELPER OF OUR FAITH IN GOD

"Likewise the Spirit also helpeth our infirmities: for we know not what we should pray for as we ought: but the Spirit itself maketh intercession for us with groanings which cannot be uttered." **Romans 8:26**

The Holy Spirit is our comforter, who is responsible for helping our infirmities, correct, instruct, and guide us according to God's original purpose for our lives. He convicts us of sin, of righteousness, and of judgment in life. The Holy spirit communicates with our spirit. "The Spirit itself beareth witness with our spirit, that we are the children of God." (Romans 8:16) As believers, we grow by learning to listen to the voice of the Holy Spirit in our faith. Being led by the Holy Spirit is the unique identifier to all believers. We obtain the help of the Holy Spirit in faith only.

~ARE YOU BEING LED BY THE HOLY SPIRIT?

Unless we are in compliance with word of God, otherwise The Holy Spirit won't help us in life. We are told *"For as many as are led by the Spirit of God, they are the sons of God."* Romans 8:16

If we must obtain help from above we must allow the Holy Spirit to direct, and guide our action in life. *Remember "There is no man that hath power over the spirit to retain the spirit..."* **(Eccl 8:8)** We must embrace yielding to the Holy spirit for direction, instruction, correction, and comfort. ***I pray Father I yield myself to you today. Direct, correct, reprove, and instruct me in Jesus Mighty Name.***

PUT YOUR FAITH TO WORK

It is my desire for you to take time out and think properly. Ask yourself what am I suppose to do? And how do I do it? I pray God to lead you in Jesus mighty name. You must put your faith to work! Amen.

Chapter 3   Understanding The Help of Faith

CONCLUSION

Although Faith in God means believing in God's word to validate and make good His promise. This includes us taking genuine steps in life towards actualizing our desired future and heart desire.

It is written *" Yea, a man may say, Thou hast faith, and I have works: shew me thy faith without thy works, and I will shew thee my faith by my works."* (James 2:18) As we conclude in this book, it is time to take action in life. Perhaps you might come up with an excuse that I do not have the capital or the resources.

It is written "For as the body without the spirit is dead, so faith without works is dead also." James 2:26

My intention is not for this book to become like a story book rather let this book help, move us into taking decisive action concerning our future." Arise ye, and depart; for this is not your rest: because it is polluted, it shall destroy you, even with a sore destruction." (Micah 2:10) In my opinion, nothing moves around you until we decide and take action in life. You are where you find yourself today because of the previous actions you took some time ago.

"Therefore if any man be in Christ, he is a new creature: old things are passed away; behold, all things are become new. Now repeat this Prayer after me." 2 Cor 5:17

Say Lord Jesus, I accept you today, as my Lord and my savior, forgive me of my sins wash me with your blood. Right now, I believe, I am sanctified, I am save, I am free, I am free from the Power of sin to serve the Lord Jesus. Thank you Lord for saving me. Amen.

Congratulations: You are now...

A BORN AGAIN CHRISTIAN.

Again I say to you—

CONGRATULATIONS!

What must I do to determine my divine visitation?

To determine divine visitation you must be born again! The word says, *"As many as received him, to them gave He power to become the sons of God. Even to them that believe on his name."* (John 1:12)

To qualify for divine visitation, do the following with sincerity—

1) Acknowledge that you are a sinner and that He died for you. (Romans 3:23)

2) Repent of your sins. (Acts 3:19, Luke 13:5, 2 Peter 3:9)

Chapter 3   Understanding The Help of Faith

3) Believe in your heart that Jesus died for your sin. (Romans 10:10)

4) Confess Jesus as the Lord over your life. (Romans 10:10, Acts 2:21)

"Therefore if any man be in Christ, he is a new creature: old things are passed away; behold, all things are become new." (2 Cor 5:17)

Now repeat this Prayer after me

Say Lord Jesus, I accept you today, as my Lord and my savior, forgive me of my sins wash me with your blood. Right now, I believe, I am sanctified, I am save, I am free, I am free from the Power of sin to serve the Lord Jesus. Thank you Lord for saving me. Amen.

Congratulations: You are now...

A BORN AGAIN CHRISTIAN.

Again I say to you—

CONGRATULATIONS!

I will encourage you to join a bible believing church or join us on our weekly and Sunday worship services at 343 Sanford Avenue Newark New Jersey 07106.

WISDOM KEYS

— Every Productive Society is a society heading to the top.

— Millions of Nigerians run away from Nigeria, very few Nigerians stay in Nigeria.

— My decision to return Nigeria is the will of God for my life.

— My short coming in America after 18 years, trained me to be wise, to think, reflect and reason appropriately.

— If you train your mind to reason it will train your hands to earn money.

— It is absurd to use the money of the heathen to build the kingdom of the living God.

— Every Ministry reveals its agenda and goal either at the beginning or at the end. Be careful of your life it is your first Ministry.

— The average American mind is conditioned for a continual quest to get new things and (discard the former) and throw away old things.

— When I considered well, my BMW jeep became my initial deposit for the work of the ministry in Nigeria.

— Money will never fall from any tree.

— Everyone is waiting for you to change your mind until you change your thinking nothing changes around you.

— Multiple academic degrees in other discipline gave me the chance to think, reflect and reason.

— What so everyone are thinking and reflecting at the moment reveals you to the time and the now factor .

— All events and intents are the product of precise thought processes, accurate reason every event is designed for a designated timeline.

— Wisdom is your ability to think, to create and invent. If you can think wise enough you will come out of penury.

— The distance between you and success is your creative ability to think reason and reflect accurate.

— Success is the result of hard work, commitment resolve and determination learning from past mistakes and failing.

— If you organize your mind you have organized your life and destiny.

— There is a thin line between success and failure. If you look above and beyond you are on your way to success.

— Wealth is your ability to think, power is your ability to reason and success is your ability to be informed.

— If you can make use of your mind by thinking and reasoning God will make use of your life and destiny.

— Think and Be Great.

— Reflect, Reason, Think and Be Great.

— Famous people are born of woman.

— That you will make it is your intention; that you will survive is your resolve, that you will succeed with changes is your determination, personal efforts and hard work.

— No man was born a failure. Lack of vision is the end product of failure.

— Working with mental patients encourages and aspire me to be a productive observant and dedicated to my assignment.

— Successful people are not magicians, it is the will power combined with hard work, and determination and a resolve to succeed that make them succeed.

— In the unequivocal state of the mind, intention is not a location or a position it is the state of the mind.

Chapter 3   Understanding The Help of Faith

— So many people think, that they think. The mind is used to think, reflect, and reason. You will remain blind with your eye open until you can see with your mind by thinking.

— There is no favoritism in accurate and precise calculation.

— Although knowledge is power, information is the key and gateway to a great future.

— It will take the hand of God to move the hand of man.

— With the backing of the great wise God, nothing will disconnect you from your inheritance.

— As long as you have wisdom and understanding of God, Satan and evil cannot manipulate your life and destiny.

— You have come this far by yourself judgment and decision you have made in the past, now lean and listen to God for another dimension of greatness.

— Great people are common people it is extra ordinary effort and the price of sacrifice that produces greatness.

— As a mental direct care worker I saw a great pastor and a motivational speaker within myself.

— Menial job does not reduce your self-worth, until you resolve to achieve greatness see greatness in all you do; you will never count in your community.

— The principle of Jesus will solve your gambling and addiction problems.

— The man of Jesus will lead you into heaven,

— Everyone have their self-appraisal and what they think about you. Until you discover yourself other opinion about you will alter the real you.

— Supervisors and directors are just a position in the chain of command in a work place. Never allow your supervisor hierarchy to alter your opinion about yourself.

— Everyone can come out of debt if they make up their mind.

— That I am not a decision maker at work does not diminish my contribution to my world.

— Although it appears like it was a poor decision to accept a direct care employment at a psychiatric hospital as I reflect of my nine years of experience, it became apparent that I have learnt and experienced enough for my next assignment in life.

Chapter 3   Understanding The Help of Faith

— Self-encouragement and determination is a resolve of the heart.

— If you are determined to make a difference, and do the things that make a difference you will eventually make a difference.

— Good things do not come easy.

— Short cuts will cut your life short.

— Those who look ahead move ahead.

— Life is all about making an impact. In your life time strive to make an impact in your community.

— Make friends and connect with people who are moving ahead of you in life.

— If you can look around well you have come a long way in your life, made a lot of difference and realized a lot of success in life.

— If you are my old friend, hurry up to reach out to me before I become a stranger to you.

— Everything I am blessed with inspirations from God, that change my definition and interpretation of the world around me.

— I thought I was stagnant and lonely until I looked around and noticed my children running around and my wife cooking.

— At 40 I resigned my Job to seek the Lord forever.

— My ministry took a drastic rise to the top when the wisdom of God visited me with knowledge and understanding.

— You will be a better person, if you understand the characteristics of your personality – your mood swings, attitudes, and habits.

— It is the seed of love you sow into the heart of a child and a woman that you reap in due time.

— Love is not selfish, love share everything including the concealed secrets of the mind.

— As long as you have a prayer life and a bible; you will never feel lonely, rejected, and idle in the race of life.

— When good friends disconnect from you, let them go, they might have seen something new in a different direction.

— Confidence in yourself and in God is the only way to bring you out of captivity.

Chapter 3   Understanding The Help of Faith

— Never train a child to waste his/her time.

— The mind is the greatest assets of a great future.

— You walk by common sense run by principles and fly by instruction.

— Those who fly in flight of life fly alone.

— Up in the air you are alone. No one can toll you accept the compass of knowledge and information.

— I have seen a towing vehicle I have seen a towing ship I have never seen a tolling airplane.

— I exercise my judgment and make a decision every minute of the day.

— Decisions are crucial, critical and vital with reference to your future.

— So many people wish for a great future. You can only work towards a great future.

— Your celebrity status began when you discovered your talent. What are you good at? Work at it with all commitment.

— Prayers will sustain you but the wisdom of God will prosper you.

— When I met Oyedepo, his teachings changed my perspective. But when I met Ibiyeomie; His teaching changed my perception.

— I will be successful in ministry if only I concentrate and focus my energy in the work of the ministry.

— It took the late Dr. Vincent Pearle Norman's book to open my mind towards kingdom success.

CHAPTER 4

PRAYER OF SALVATION

"Neither is there salvation in any other: for there is none other name under heaven given among men, whereby we must be saved."
Acts 4:12

Salvation, simply means deliverance of our soul from sin and the destruction of the devil. If we must make it with God in eternity, we must genuinely recognize what we need to do in righteousness to live a new life with Jesus Christ.

What must I do to determine my salvation?

To be saved we must be born again!
The word says as many as received him, to them gave He power to become the sons of God. Even to them that believe on his name.

To qualify for divine visitation, do the following with sincerity—

1) Acknowledge that you are a sinner and that He died for you. (Romans 3:23)

2) Repent of your sins. (Acts 3:19, Luke 13:5, 2 Peter 3:9)

3) Believe in your heart that Jesus died for your sin. (Romans 10:10)

4) Confess Jesus as the Lord over your life. (Romans 10:10, Acts 2:21)

Now repeat this Prayer after me

Say Lord Jesus, I accept you today, as my Lord and my savior, forgive me of my sins wash me with your blood. Right now, I believe, I am sanctified, I am save, I am free, I am free from the Power of sin to serve the Lord Jesus. Thank you Lord for saving me. Amen.

Congratulations: You are now...

A BORN AGAIN CHRISTIAN.

Again I say to you—

CONGRATULATIONS!

I adjure you to watch the Spirit of God bear witness with your Spirit confirming His word with signs following. The word says The Spirit itself beareth witness with our spirit, that we are the children of God.

MIRACLE CARE OUTREACH

*"...But that the members should have
the same care one for another"*
1 Corinthians 12:25

     We are all members of the body of Christ. Jesus commanded us to love our neighbor as ourselves. This includes caring for one another as a member of one body. True love is expressed in caring and giving. The word says for God so Love He gave....

     Reach out to someone in need of Jesus, help someone in crisis find Christ. Look out and prove your love to Jesus by caring and inviting your friends and associates to find Jesus the Healer.

     Invite your friends to our Home Care Cell Fellowship (Miracle chapel Intl Satellite fellowship) In the USA at 33 Schley Street Newark New Jersey 07112. Home Care Cell fellowship Group meets every Tuesday at 6:00pm-7:00pm.

     If you are in Nigeria—**MIRACLE OF GOD MINISTRIES**, aka "**MIRACLE CHAPEL INTL**" Mpama –Egbu-Owerri Imo state Nigeria.

LIFE IS NOT ALL ABOUT DURATION— BUT ITS ALL ABOUT DONATION

What does the above statement mean?....

Life consists not in accumulation of material wealth. (Luke 12:15) But it's all about liberality...i.e., what you can give and share with others. (Proverbs 11:25) When you live for others, you live forever—because you out-live your generation by the legacy you live behind after you depart into glory to be with the Lord. But when you live to yourself, when you are reduced to SELF—you are easily forgotten when you die and depart in glory.

Permit me to admonish you today to live your life to be a blessing to a soul connected to you today. I want you to know that so many souls are connected and looking up to you, and through you so many souls will be saved and rescued from destruction. Will you disciple someone today to find Jesus Christ?

As a genuine Christian; it is your duty to evangelize Jesus Christ to all you meet on your way. Jesus is still in the healing business—Jesus is still doing miracles from time of old to now. Therefore, tell someone about Jesus Christ today, disciple and bring them to Church. *Philip findeth Nathanael...* (John 1:45)

Please to prove the sincerity of your love for God today; please become a soul winner. The dignity of your Christianity is hidden in your boldness to proclaim and evangelize Jesus Christ to all you meet on your way. There is a question mark on the integrity of your Christianity until you become a life soul winner. Invite someone to join us worship the Lord Jesus this coming Sunday. Amen.

MIRACLE OF GOD MINISTRIES

PILLARS OF THE COMMISSION

We Believe Preach and Practice the following:

1) We believe and preach Salvation to every living human being

2) We believe and preach Repentance and forgiveness of sins

3) We believe and preach the baptism of the Holy Spirit and Spiritual gifts

4) We believe and teach the Prosperity

5) We believe and preach Divine Healing and Miracles (Signs &Wonder)

6) We believe and preach Faith

7) We believe and proclaim the Power of God (Supernatural)

8) We believe and proclaim Praise& Worship to God

9) We believe and preach Wisdom

10) We believe and preach Holiness (Consecration)

11) We believe and preach Vision

12) We believe and teach the Word of God

13) We believe and teach Success

14) We believe and practice Prayer

15) We believe and teach Deliverance

These 15 stones form the Pillars of Our Commission. Become part of this church family and follow this great move of God.

MY HEART FELT PRAYER FOR YOU

It is not only my desire, but my uttermost vision that you encounter the Lord Jesus Christ as your personal Lord and savior. You must be born again. As ruthless as it may sound today, it is my ministry to see you saved and engrafted into the kingdom of God. For the most part most folks does not understand "Salvation" and what it means to be "saved." We all must consciously make genuine plan for heaven. Unless you plan to make heaven, you will not make heaven.

Now let me Pray for you:

Holy Spirit of God, we give you thanks and praise. Lord I pray that the eyes of our understanding may be opened today. May we put faith to work by taking action in our lives, in the mighty Name of Jesus. Amen.

IT'S TIME TO TAKE ACTION IN LIFE

Unless we agree to take action nothing changes for us in life. Most lazy Christians will only pray and fast. The truth is prayer and fasting is not a substitute of breakthrough in life. Unless you do the right thing at the right place and at the right time, there is no favoritism with God. God is a God of wisdom and knowledge. We must therefore take advantage of our God given wisdom and understanding in life. We must genuinely use God's given wisdom and understanding to take fruitful action in life concerning our future.

Unless we take action in life, we cannot overcome the wicked one. One man said if we fail to plan we have planned to fail. I admonish you to take action beginning today in your life. Action oriented people *put their faith to work in life.* I see you taking control of your destiny in *the mighty Name of Jesus.*

CHAPTER 5

ABOUT THE AUTHOR

Rev Franklin N Abazie is the founding and Presiding Pastor of Miracle of God Ministries with headquarters in Newark, New Jersey USA and a branch church in Owerri- Imo State Nigeria. He is following the footsteps of one of his mentors, Oral Roberts (Healing Evangelist) of the blessed memory. The Lord passed Oral Roberts healing mantle two days before he went to be with the Lord at age 91 into the hand of healing evangelist-Rev Franklin N Abazie in a vision.

In all his services the Power and Presence of God is present to heal all in his audience. He is an ordained man of God with a Healing Ministry reviving the healing and miracle ministry of Jesus Christ of Nazareth.

Pastor Franklin N Abazie, is called by God with a unique mandate: **"THE MOMENT IS DUE TO IMPACT YOUR WORLD THROUGH THE REVIVAL OF THE HEALING & MIRACLE MINISTRY OF JESUS CHRIST OF NAZARETH**

"I AM SENDING YOU TO RESTORE HEALTH UNTO THEE AND I WILL HEAL THEE OF THY WOUNDS. SAID THE LORD OF HOST"

Rev. Abazie is a gifted ardent Teacher of the word of God who operates also in the office of a Prophet, generating and attracting undeniable signs & wonders, special miracles and healings, with apostolic fireworks of the Holy Ghost. He is the founding and presiding senior Pastor of this fast growing Healing ministry. He has written over 86 inspirational, healing and transforming books covering almost all aspect of divine healing and life. He is happily married and blessed with children.

Chapter 5   About The Author

BOOKS BY REV FRANKLIN N ABAZIE

1) *The Outcome of Faith*
2) *Understanding the secret of prevailing Prayers*
3) *Commanding Abundance*
4) *Understanding the secret of the man God uses*
5) *Activating my due Season*
6) *Overcoming Divine Verdicts*
7) *The Outcome of Divine Wisdom*
8) *Understanding God's Restoration Mandate*
9) *Walking in the Victory and Authority of the truth*
10) *Gods Covenant Exemption*
11) *Destiny Restoration Pillars*
12) *Provoking Acceptable Praise*
13) *Understanding Divine Judgment*
14) *Activating Angelic Re-enforcement*
15) *Provoking Un-Merited Favor*
16) *The Benefits of the Speaking faith*
17) *Understanding Divine Arrangement*
18) *Put your faith to work*
19) *Developing a positive attitude in life*
20) *The Power of Prevailing faith*
21) *Inexplicable faith*
22) *The intellectual components of Redemption.*
23) *Dominating Controlling Spirit*
24) *Understanding Divine Prosperity*
25) *Understanding the secret of the man God Uses*
26) *Retaining Your Inheritance*
27) *Never give up hope*
28) *Commanding Angelic Escorts*
29) *The winner's faith*
30) *Understanding Your Guardian Angels*
31) *Overcoming the Dominion of Sin*
32) *Understanding the Voice of God*
33) *The Outstanding benefits of the Anointing*

34) The Audacity of the Blood of Jesus
35) Walking in the Reality of the Anointing
36) The Mystery of Divine supply
37) Understanding Your Harvest Season
38) Activating Your Success Buttons
39) Overcoming the forces of Darkness
40) Overcoming the devices of the devil
41) Overcoming Demonic agents
42) Overcoming the sorrows of failure
43) Rejecting the Sorrows of failure
44) Resisting the Sorrows of Poverty
45) The Restoring broken Marriages.
46) Redeeming Your Days
47) The force of Vision
48) Overcoming the forces of ignorance
49) Understanding the sacrifice of small beginning
50) The might of small beginning
51) Praying in the Spirit
52) Dominating controlling Spirits
53) Breaking the shackles of the curse of the law
54) Covenant keys to answered prayers
55) Wisdom for Signs & Wonders
56) Wisdom for generational Impact
57) Wisdom for Marriage Stability
58) Understanding the number of your Days
59) Enforcing Your Kingdom Rights
60) Escaping the traps of immoralities
61) Escaping the trap of Poverty
62) Accessing Biblical Prosperity
63) Accessing True Riches in Christ
64) Silencing the Voice of the Accuser
65) Overcoming the forces of oppositions
66) Quenching the voice of the avenger
67) Silencing demonic Prediction & Projection
68) Silencing Your Mocker
69) Understanding the Power of the Holy Ghost

Chapter 5   About The Author

70) Understanding the baptism of Power
71) The Mystery of the Blood of Jesus
72) Understanding the Mystery of Sanctification
73) Understanding the Power of Holiness
74) Praying in the spirit
75) Activating the Forces of Vengeance
76) Appreciating the Mystery of Restoration
77) Covenant Keys to Answered Prayers
78) Engaging the mystery of the blood
79) Commanding the Power of the Speaking faith
80) Uprooting the forces against Your Rising
81) Overcoming mere success syndrome
82) Understanding Divine Sentence
83) Understanding the Mystery of Praise
84) Understanding the Author of Faith
85) The Mystery of the finisher of faith
86) Where is your trust?

MIRACLE OF GOD MINISTRIES

NIGERIA CRUSADE 2012

MIRACLE OF GOD MINISTRIES

NIGERIA CRUSADE 2012

MIRACLE OF GOD MINISTRIES

NIGERIA CRUSADE 2012

www.ingramcontent.com/pod-product-compliance
Lightning Source LLC
Chambersburg PA
CBHW071540080526
44588CB00011B/1735